# Girl's Guide to
## Basic Cooking

# Girl's Guide to
# Basic Cooking

Lesley Pagett

NEW HOLLAND

# Contents

# Introduction

Every girl needs a repertoire of fabulous, flavourful and nutritious recipes at her fingertips. These are the recipes that you'll make again and again, either because they're fast to cook and you can feed yourself quickly; they're inexpensive to make and therefore worth the extra prep time that may be involved in creating them; or because you absolutely love them.

Learning to cook is a key skill to master. Once learnt, it's never forgotten, and with lots of practise it can become second nature. It does take time to learn though, so if you're a novice, applaud yourself for having a go, learn from your mistakes, retain your patience and sense of humour, and feel proud of every success. We all learn to cook in different ways and for different reasons. Perhaps you were fortunate to be brought up in an environment where learning to cook with mum or gran was part of everyday life? Maybe, you weren't so fortunate and learning to cook feels like a daunting prospect? Perhaps you have friends who enjoy good food and have developed a palate for fine flavours and now want to create your own? The great thing to remember, is that we can all learn to cook no matter what our starting point.

For many people, cooking can become a passion, the key to a social life, and one of life's great pleasures. For others, it's a chore and a necessity once we've had

our fill of standard take-out dishes and exhausted the supermarket ready meals. Sooner or later our tastebuds will tell us that it's time for a change, and often that change means learning to cook.

There's good reason to learn too. Home-cooked food can be vastly superior to ready prepared supermarket dishes. It's significantly cheaper to make your own dishes, and your repertoire will broaden. Then there's the advantage that home-cooked fare is more filling and satisfying to eat than ready made.

With all these thoughts to the fore, *Girl's Guide to Basic Cooking* has been designed with the novice cook in mind. Here you'll find a wide range of dishes that are instantly appealing. From soups to curries and roast dishes, there's something here suitable for every palate and to whet every appetite. These are the recipes that we're all familiar with, and the tried-and-tested dishes that have stood the test of time. Home-made spaghetti bolognese, lasagne, fishcakes, and roast chicken are just a few of the recipes that feature.

The collection has been arranged in chapters according to type of dish or main ingredient. Maybe you want to make soup for a packed lunch or a first course? Perhaps you'd like to cook a roast dinner for friends, or want to try your hand at cooking fish? Whatever your requirement, a comprehensive list of ingredients is provided for each recipe using standard imperial and metric measures. The measures are not interchangeable though, so if you start measuring out your quantities in imperial then stick with that set of measures to the end of the recipe.

Each recipe features a concise method that explains in detail every stage of making. And since this is a beginner's guide, none of the instructions are particularly complex and all use terminology that is standard to every cookbook. From frying and grilling, to poaching and roasting (and not forgetting pudding), this pleasing collection of recipes will guide you through each technique to help you produce timeless classic dishes that you can be proud of. For many recipes there are photographs of the finished dish to inspire your culinary endeavours.

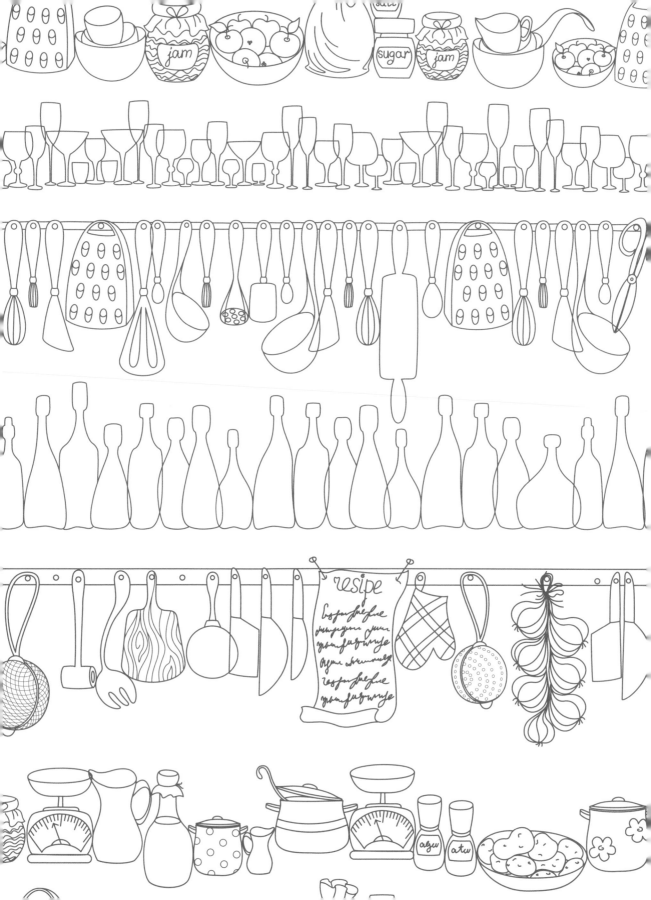

# Soups

# Cream of Chicken Soup

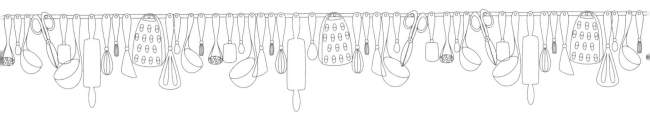

## INGREDIENTS

60 g (2 oz) butter

4 tablespoons plain
(all-purpose) flour

1.2 litres (2 pints) chicken
stock

600 ml (1 pint) scalded milk
(or 300 ml (½ pint milk) and
300 ml (½ pint milk) single
(light) cream)

1 chicken breast, shredded

1 small stalk celery, finely
chopped

few drops tabasco sauce

salt and freshly ground black
pepper, to taste

2 egg yolks

fresh chives, chopped, to
serve

## METHOD

Melt the butter in a large pan over medium heat, stir in the flour
until smooth and cook for about 1 minute. Add the chicken stock,
slowly, stirring continuously until smooth. Stir continuously over
medium heat until boiling.

Add the scalded milk, chicken, celery, tabasco sauce and salt
and pepper and bring to the boil. Reduce the heat and simmer,
covered, for 5 minutes.

In a bowl, beat the egg yolks well with a fork, then pour into
a warmed tureen. Pour the soup very slowly over the egg yolks,
stirring all the time with a wooden spoon.

Garnish with some fresh chives. Serve immediately.

serves
4

# Cream of Mushroom Soup

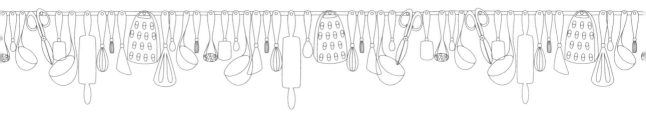

## INGREDIENTS

250 g (9 oz) mushrooms

125 g (4½ oz) butter

½ teaspoon salt

freshly ground black pepper, to taste

3 garlic cloves, finely chopped

1.2 litres (2 pints) chicken stock

150 ml (5 fl oz) fresh cream, at room temperature

garlic-flavoured croutons, to serve

parsley, chopped, to serve

## METHOD

Set aside a few mushrooms for the garnish.

Wipe the mushrooms with a damp cloth, then thinly slice them. In a frying pan, heat the butter to sizzling, then fry the mushrooms with the salt and a generous grind of pepper. Leave to cool, then purée in a blender or food processor with the garlic and 250 ml (8 fl oz) stock.

Pour the remaining stock into a large pan. Add the purée and heat the soup to simmering point. Stir in the cream. Add the reserved mushroom slices and simmer for 5 minutes. Taste and adjust the seasoning, if necessary.

Serve hot with garlic-flavoured croutons and a sprinkle of parsley.

serves
4

# Leek, Potato and Bacon Soup

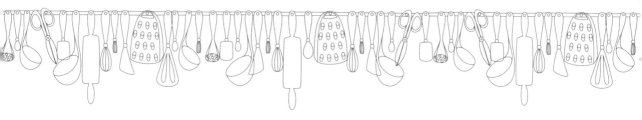

## INGREDIENTS

2.5 kg (5½ lb) potatoes, peeled
and cut into chunks

2 leeks, sliced into 3 cm
(1¼ in) rings

500 g (1 lb 2 oz) bacon,
chopped

salt and freshly ground black
pepper, to taste

300 ml (½ pint) sour cream

2 or 3 shallots, chopped

¼ bunch coriander (cilantro),
chopped

## METHOD

Place the potatoes in a large pan with enough water to cover.
Bring the water to the boil and cook the potatoes for about
10 minutes, or until soft. Use a slotted spoon to remove the
potatoes to a large bowl. Retain the potato water.

Mash the potatoes with some saved water (the mixture should
have the consistency of thick soup).

Return the mashed potatoes to the pan with the leek and
bacon and simmer until the leek is soft and the bacon is cooked.
Season with salt and pepper.

In a bowl, mix the sour cream and shallots. Serve hot,
garnished with coriander and sour cream and shallots.

serves
4-6

# Pumpkin Soup

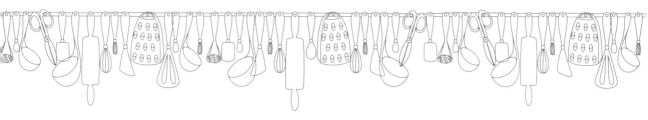

## INGREDIENTS

60 g (2 oz) butter

1 white onion, finely chopped

600 ml (1 pint) chicken stock

500 g (1 lb 2 oz) pumpkin, peeled, seeded and cut into 5 mm (¼ in) chunks

600 ml (1 pint) hot milk

¼ teaspoon ground allspice (see note)

salt and freshly ground black pepper, to taste

125 ml (4 fl oz) double (heavy) cream

finely chopped parsley and garlic-flavoured croutons, to garnish

## METHOD

Melt the butter in a large pan then gently fry the onion for 10 minutes, or until soft.

Add the chicken stock and bring to the boil.

Add the pumpkin to the stock and simmer until tender, about 30 minutes. Leave to cool.

Purée the pumpkin in a food processor or blender. Return the soup to the pan, add the hot milk, ground allspice, salt and pepper, and heat gently. Add the thickened cream just before serving.

Serve garnished with parsley and garlic-flavoured croutons.

Note: Allspice is the dried berry of the pimiento tree. The dried berries are dark brown and are available whole or ground. The whole berries are used in pickles, preserves and chutney and when ground as a flavouring in cakes, soups and meat dishes.

serves
8

# Tomato Soup

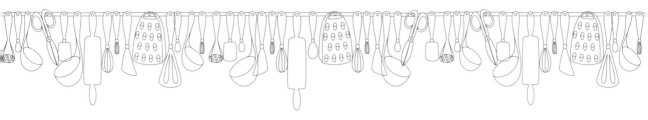

## INGREDIENTS

2 rashers (strips) bacon, chopped

30 g (1 oz) butter (optional)

2 kg (4½ lb) ripe tomatoes, skinned and chopped (see note)

1 onion, chopped

1 carrot, peeled and grated (shredded)

1 stick celery, chopped

900 ml (1½ pints) chicken stock

salt and black pepper, to taste

bouquet garni (see note)

## METHOD

Dry fry the bacon in a large pan, add the butter (if using) and once sizzling, toss in the tomatoes, onion, carrot and celery and cook until softened. Do not allow the bacon or onion to brown. Add the stock, salt and pepper and bouquet garni, then cover and simmer gently for about 35 minutes. Adjust the seasoning. Leave to cool. Process in a food processor or blender in batches then reheat just before serving.

Notes: Bouquet garni is a bundle of herbs tied together with string. Commonly used to flavour soups, sauces and stews. The herbs are usually parsley, thyme and bay leaf.

To skin a tomato, cut a cross in one side of the skin using a sharp knife. Put in a heatproof bowl and pour over boiling water to cover. Set aside for a few minutes until the skin starts to life. Remove from the bowl with a slotted spoon and when cool enough to handle, peel the skin from the tomato.

serves
4

# Seafood Chowder

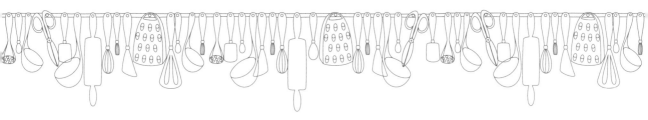

## INGREDIENTS

500 g (1 lb 2 oz) marinara mix (fish pieces, shelled shrimp (prawns), oysters, scallops, crab meat)

750 ml (1¼ pints) water

30 g (1 oz) butter

1 onion, sliced

1 potato, sliced

½ teaspoon saffron (optional)

salt, to taste

250 ml (8 fl oz) milk

60–125 ml (2–4 fl oz) fresh cream

salt and freshly ground black pepper, to taste

1 tablespoon parsley, finely chopped, to garnish

Crusty bread, to serve

## METHOD

Poach the seafood in a large pan of salted water over medium-low heat until just tender. Strain and retain the liquid. Remove and discard any skin or bones from the fish and set aside. Set aside the seafood.

Melt the butter in a pan and sauté the onion and potato slices for 2 minutes. Add the strained stock, saffron and salt. Simmer for 20 minutes, then purée in a blender or food processor until smooth.

Return the soup to the pan, add the milk and bring to the boil. Add the cream and seafood and season to taste. Heat gently but do not boil.

Garnish with parsley and serve with crusty bread.

serves
4-6

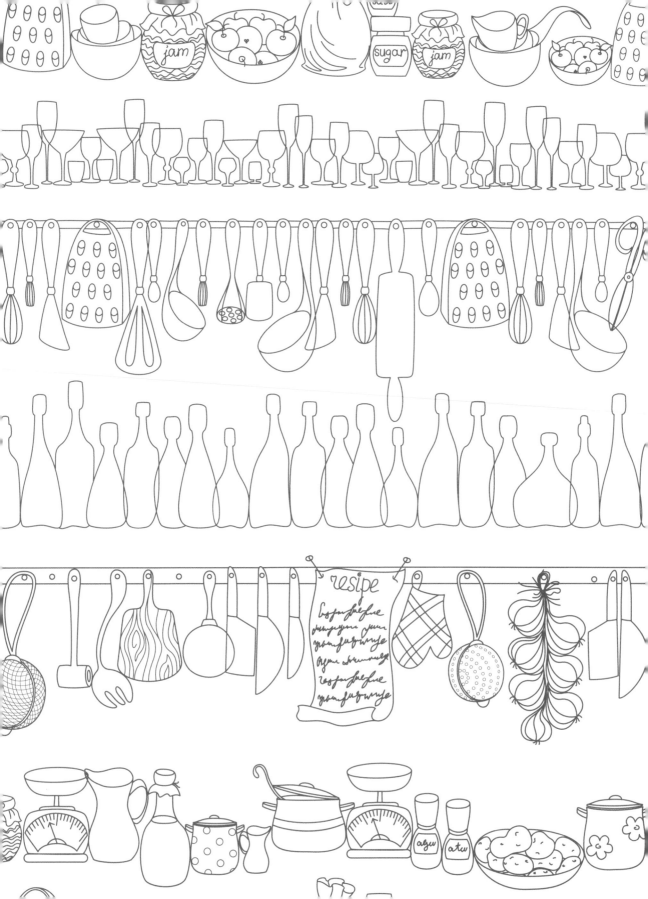

# Salads

# Avocado Orange Salad

## INGREDIENTS

1 lettuce, washed and leaves
  separated
2 avocados, peeled, pit
  removed and flesh sliced
2 oranges, cut into segments
2 tablespoons slivered
  almonds, toasted

## FOR THE DRESSING

2 tablespoons orange juice
2 tablespoons olive oil
1 tablespoon white wine
  vinegar
1 teaspoon shallots
  (scallions), chopped
¼ teaspoon curry powder
salt and ground black pepper,
  to taste

## METHOD

To make the dressing, combine all of the ingredients in a bowl and season to taste.

Line a salad bowl with lettuce leaves. Layer the remaining leaves into the bowl. Arrange the avocados and orange segments decoratively over the lettuce.

Drizzle the dressing onto the salad, and garnish with almonds.

serves
4

# Pasta Salad

## INGREDIENTS

500 g (1 lb 2 oz) dried fusilli
pasta
1 tablespoon olive oil
½ teaspoon salt
½ red capsicum (bell pepper),
seeds and pith removed and
diced
4–6 mushrooms, sliced
4–6 shallots (scallions), finely
chopped
125 g (4½ oz) mung beans
125 g (4½ oz) sweet corn
kernels (optional)
300 ml (½ pint) mayonnaise

## METHOD

Place the pasta into a large pan of boiling water with the oil and
salt, and cook for 8 minutes, or until the pasta is *al dente*. Rinse
and strain.

Place all ingredients, except the mayonnaise, in a bowl and
toss to combine. Add the mayonnaise to taste.

serves
6-8

# Caesar Salad

## INGREDIENTS

1 garlic clove, peeled

1 cos lettuce, leaves washed and dried

1 endive, leaves washed and dried

2 tablespoons Parmesan, grated (shredded)

4 anchovy fillets, each chopped into 3–4 pieces

1 coddled egg (boiled for 1 minute)

Garlic-flavoured croutons, to serve

## METHOD

Rub the salad bowl with the peeled clove of garlic. For the dressing, put the salt, mustard, lemon juice and tabasco sauce into a bowl and stir with a wooden spoon until the salt dissolves. Add the olive oil and blend well.

Tear the salad greens into bite-sized pieces and place in a salad bowl. Scatter over the cheese and the anchovy fillets. Break in the coddled egg and toss well. Drizzle with dressing.

Just before serving, sprinkle with garlic-flavoured croutons and toss again.

serves 6-8

# Thai Beef Salad

## INGREDIENTS

6 lettuce leaves

500 g (1 lb 2 oz) beef rump
   or tenderloin, roasted and
   sliced into strips

2 garlic cloves, finely chopped

1 Spanish (Bermuda) onion,
   sliced

1 stalk lemongrass

¼ cup coriander leaves, torn

1 cup mint leaves, torn

fried onion, to garnish

1 tablespoon dried chilli
   flakes, to garnish

## FOR THE DRESSING

4 kaffir lime leaves, cut into
   strips

3 garlic cloves, finely chopped

5 green serrano chillies,
   seeded and finely chopped

1 tablespoon fish sauce (nam
   pla)

juice of 1 lime

60 g (2 oz) brown sugar

## METHOD

To make the salad dressing, combine all the ingredients in a bowl (or jar) and mix well (or put the lid on and give it a shake). To serve, arrange the lettuce leaves on a serving dish, covering the whole surface area. Place strips of beef over the lettuce and scatter over the garlic, onion, lemongrass, coriander and mint.

   Pour the dressing over the top and garnish with fried onion and chilli flakes.

serves
6

# Potato Salad

### INGREDIENTS

1 kg (2 lb 4 oz) new potatoes,
  peeled
75 ml (2½ fl oz) French
  dressing
75 g (2½ oz) cucumber, finely
  chopped
50 g (1¾ oz) celery, finely
  chopped
40 g (1¼ oz) onion, finely
  sliced
4 hard-boiled eggs, coarsely
  chopped
250 ml (8 fl oz) mayonnaise
125 ml (4 fl oz) sour cream
1 tablespoon horseradish
  relish
salt and freshly ground black
  pepper, to taste
2 bacon rashers (strips),
  cooked and finely chopped,
  to garnish

serves
6-8

### METHOD

Cook the potatoes in boiling salted water until just tender. Drain well and leave to cool just enough to be handled, then cut into small cubes.

Place the potatoes in a bowl and pour over the French dressing. Leave the potatoes to cool, then add the cucumber, celery, onion and egg.

In a bowl, combine the mayonnaise, sour cream and horseradish relish. Pour over potatoes and toss gently. Season with salt and pepper.

Garnish with bacon just before serving.

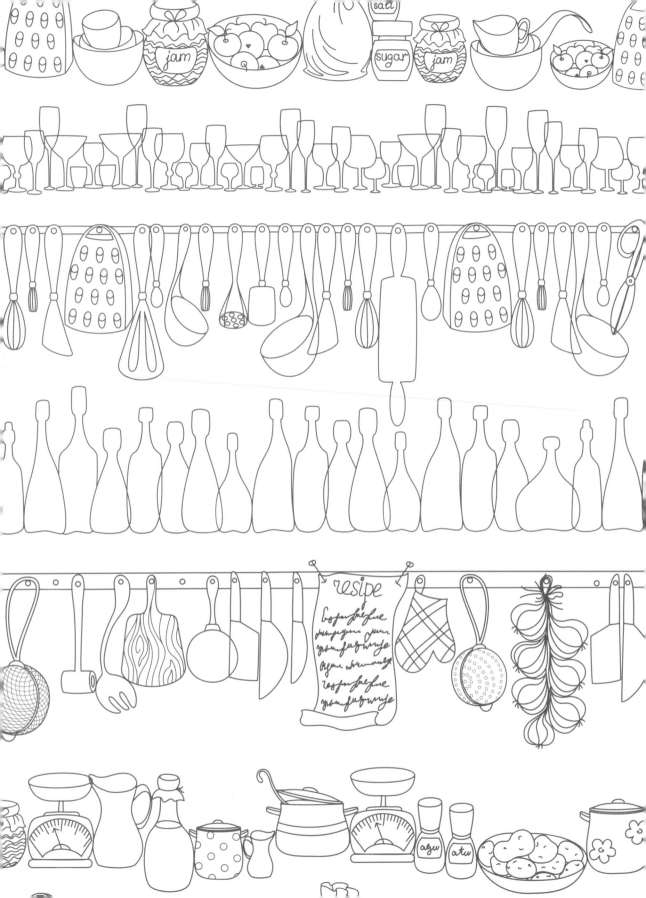

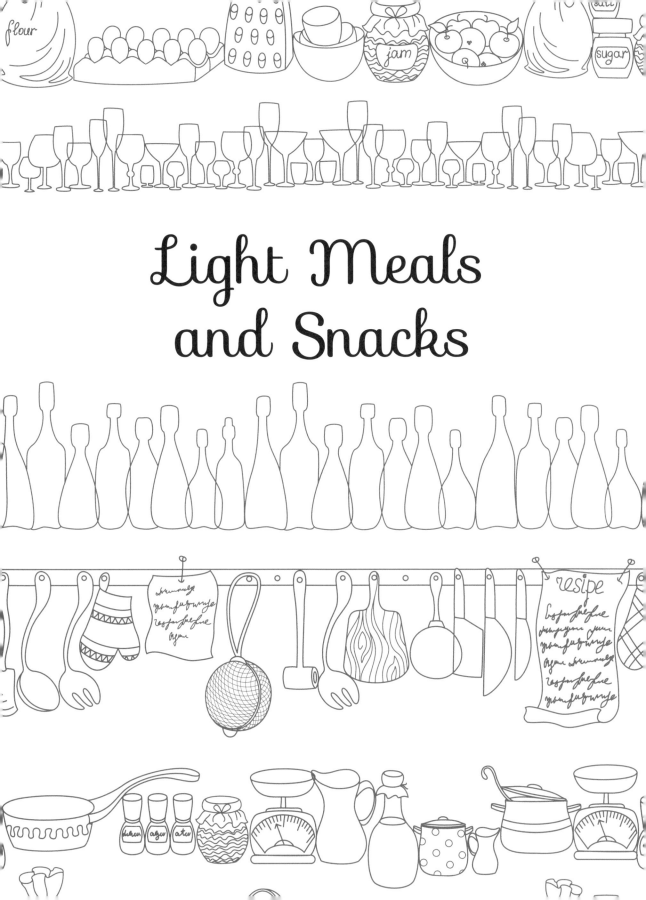

# Light Meals and Snacks

# Garlic Bread

## INGREDIENTS

1 French bread stick
2 garlic cloves, peeled and
    crushed
250 g (9 oz) butter

## METHOD

Preheat the oven to 220°C (420°F/Gas mark 7). Slice the bread almost to the bottom, being careful not to sever the slices.

In a small bowl, mash the garlic thoroughly into the butter. Spread the garlic butter generously on both sides of the bread slices. Wrap the bread loosely in aluminium foil, and bake for 10–15 minutes, until crisp and golden. Serve hot.

serves
4

# Cinnamon Toast

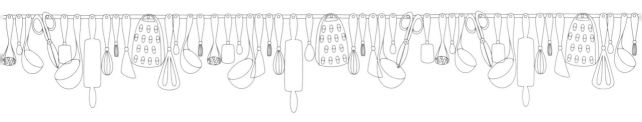

## INGREDIENTS

40 g (1¼ oz) caster (superfine)
   sugar
1 teaspoon ground cinnamon
2 slices white bread
butter, softened

## METHOD

Mix the sugar and cinnamon in a bowl.

   Toast the bread lightly on both sides and butter one side, spreading the butter right to the edges. Sprinkle each slice of toast evenly with the cinnamon and sugar mixture. Put the toast under the grill (broiler) and cook until the sugar starts to melt. Remove and serve hot.

serves
1

# French Toast

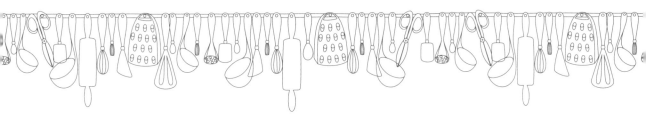

## INGREDIENTS
1–2 eggs
60 ml (2 fl oz) milk
1 tablespoons caster
  (superfine) sugar
¼ teaspoon vanilla extract
¼ teaspoon salt
butter, for frying
2 thick slices of bread

## METHOD
In a bowl, combine the eggs, milk, sugar, vanilla and salt.

Heat a little butter in a frying pan over medium heat. Dip a slice of bread into the egg mixture until the bread is completely coated and has soaked up some egg mixture. Place the bread in the frying pan and cook for 1 minute on each side, or until it is crisp and golden. Repeat with the remaining bread, until the egg mixture has all been used.

Serve hot.

serves
2

# Guacamole

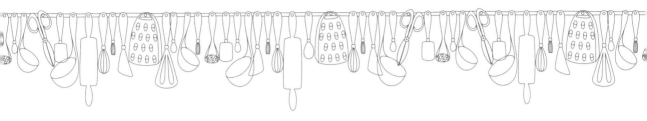

## INGREDIENTS

2 tablespoons lemon juice

2–3 tablespoons olive oil

½ clove garlic, peeled and
    crushed

salt, to taste

½ teaspoon tabasco sauce

1 large avocado, diced

2 heaped tablespoons sour
    cream

1 small onion, finely chopped

1 tomato, diced

corn chips, to serve

## METHOD

Place all the ingredients, except for the onion and tomato, in a bowl and beat together with a fork until smooth. Add the tomato and onion and mix through. Serve with corn chips.

serves
8

# Boiled Eggs

serves
1

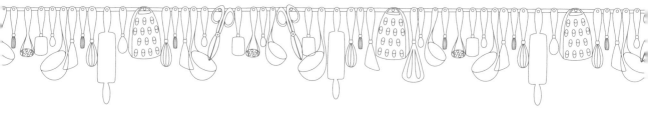

### INGREDIENTS
2 eggs
Malt vinegar, to set the egg if
the shell cracks

### METHOD
Place eggs in a pan, cover with cold water and add a dash of vinegar. Place over medium heat and bring to the boil. Boil for 3 minutes for soft-boiled eggs and 6 minutes for hard-boiled eggs. Drain and rinse under cold running water to cool slightly. This helps to remove the shell easily.

# Fried Eggs

serves
1

### INGREDIENTS
2 eggs
1 tablespoon olive oil, for
frying
hot buttered toast, to serve

### METHOD
Warm the frying pan over medium heat. Add the oil and allow to warm, then tip the pan to cover the surface. Put oiled egg rings in the frying pan, if using and crack eggs into them. Cook over a low heat for 2 minutes for sunny side up; flip the eggs and cook for another 1 minute if you prefer easy-over eggs.
   Serve hot with buttered toast.

# Scrambled Eggs on Toast

serves
1

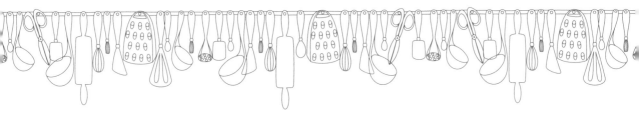

## INGREDIENTS

2 eggs

salt and freshly ground black
  pepper, to taste

fresh herbs, finely chopped
  (optional)

15 g (½ oz) butter

2 slices hot buttered toast, to
  serve

## METHOD

In a bowl, beat the eggs with salt and pepper. Add the herbs (if using).

Place 1 teaspoon of butter in a frying pan and melt over a low heat until sizzling.

Pour in the egg mixture and, using a broad wooden spatula, move the egg slowly across the pan as it thickens. When almost to the thickness desired, remove from the heat and add the remaining butter. Turn onto a plate of hot toast, and serve at once.

Variation: Finely grated (shredded) cheese can be added with the final butter.

# Omelette

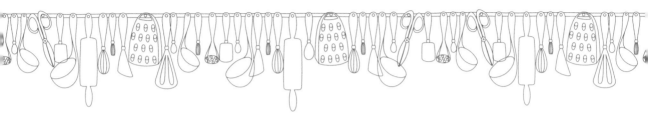

**INGREDIENTS**

3 large eggs

salt and freshly ground black
    pepper, to taste

1 tablespoon water

15 g (½ oz) butter

**METHOD**

Place a frying pan over low heat and warm slowly.

Break the eggs into a bowl, add salt and pepper, and the water. Beat to mix well.

Add butter to the frying pan. When it becomes a faint brown colour, pour in the eggs. Using a fork, and holding the pan with your hand, stir the mixture in the centre a few times, and bring the eggs from the side of the pan toward the middle. This enables any uncooked liquid to run to the sides and cook more easily.

As soon as the underside is a light golden brown, and the centre is creamy, lift the edge of the omelette nearest the pan handle, fold the omelette in half and gently roll it toward the edge.

If a filling is to be added, make it beforehand and keep it hot, then spread it on half the cooked surface and fold the side of the omelette with no filling over it. In some cases, as with chopped herbs, the filling is cooked with the egg mixture.

serves
1

# Ham and Pineapple Pizza

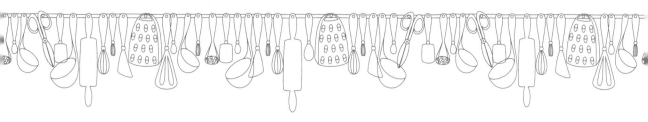

## INGREDIENTS

1 round piece Lebanese bread

3 tablespoons Italian tomato
 sauce

125 g (4½ oz) mozzarella
 cheese, grated (shredded)

### FOR THE ITALIAN TOMATO
 SAUCE

2 tablespoons olive oil

1 small onion, finely chopped

2 garlic cloves, crushed

2 x 400 g (14 oz) cans
 tomatoes, diced

½ teaspoon salt

½ teaspoon caster (superfine)
 sugar, or to taste

¼ teaspoon freshly ground
 black pepper

2 leaves basil

1 sprig oregano

1 bay leaf

1 tablespoon tomato paste

### TOPPING

100 g (3½ oz) sliced ham

1 x 400 g (14 oz) can crushed
 pineapple

## METHOD

Preheat the oven to 200°C/400°F/Gas mark 6. Place the bread on a pizza plate or baking sheet.

To make the Italian tomato sauce, in a large pan, heat the oil. Add the onion and garlic and cook for 5–6 minutes, stirring until the onion is translucent. Add the other ingredients. Return to the heat and bring to the boil. Reduce the heat, cover, and simmer for 45 minutes, stirring occasionally. Purée the sauce in a blender or food processor.

Spread the bread very thinly with the tomato sauce. Sprinkle with half the cheese. This is the basic pizza base.

Cut the ham slices into pieces about 1 cm (½ in) square. Drain the pineapple of juice. Place the ham on top of the cheese, then add the pineapple pieces. Cover with the rest of the cheese.

Bake until the cheese turns golden brown, about 10 minutes, and serve.

serves
2

# Hamburger and Fries

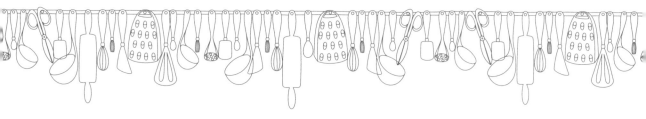

## INGREDIENTS

1 small onion, grated
  (shredded)
500 g (1 lb 2 oz) minced
  (ground) steak
3 tablespoons plain
  (all-purpose) flour, plus
  another 125 g (4½ oz)
60 ml (2 fl oz) milk
60 ml (2 fl oz) oil
6 hamburger buns

## FOR THE FRIES

6 large potatoes
vegetable oil, for deep-frying
salt, to taste

serves
6

## METHOD

To make the fries, peel the potatoes and cut into chips. Place in a large bowl and cover with ice cold water for at least 30 minutes. Dry thoroughly in a clean tea towel.

Heat the oil until very hot—a 2.5 cm (1 in) cube of bread will brown in 1 minute when the oil is hot enough. Place the dry fries in a frying basket and lower into the oil. The fries should be completely covered. Fry until tender but not brown, about 10 minutes. Remove the fries from the oil and drain. Set aside until just before serving time.

To make the burgers, mix the onion and meat in a bowl using a wooden spoon. Mix in the flour. Pour over the milk and stir well until thoroughly combined.

Place the extra flour in a small bowl. Make a heaped tablespoon of the meat mixture into a ball and roll it in the flour until coated. Put on a plate and flatten it slightly. Continue until all the meat is used.

Pour the oil into a frying pan and place over a medium heat. When the oil starts to bubble, gently place the hamburger patties in the pan. Cook until the base of the burgers are brown, then flip them over and cook until they are brown on the other side. Drain the patties on absorbent paper.

Reheat the chip oil and cook the fries until golden, crisp and slightly puffy. Drain well, sprinkle with salt, and serve immediately.

To serve, place the patties on hamburger buns and add tomato sauce, sliced cheese, and salad ingredients of your choice.

# Quiche

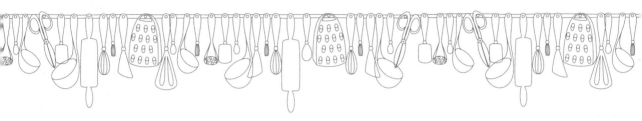

## FOR THE PASTRY

250 g (9 oz) self-raising
(self-rising) flour
175 g (6 oz) hard butter,
grated (shredded)
1 egg yolk
60 ml (2 fl oz) cold milk

## FOR THE FILLING

625 ml (generous pint) milk
3 eggs
3 spring onions (scallions),
chopped
125 g (4½ oz) ham, chopped
125 g (4½ oz) cheese, grated
(shredded)

## METHOD

Preheat the oven to 200°C/400°F/Gas mark 6.

To make the pastry, sift the flour into a large bowl and add
the butter. Mix with your fingertips until the mixture resembles
breadcrumbs. Use your fingertips to break up large lumps. Make
a hollow in the centre and drop in the egg yolk. Mix again with
your fingertips.

Pour in the milk, a little at a time, until you can make a ball
of pastry that sticks together. On a floured surface, roll out the
pastry until it is 5 mm (¼ in) thick. Place the pastry in a flan ring
or pie dish and trim off the edges. Put it into the refrigerator,
covered, for about 30 minutes.

To make the filling, pour the milk into a large bowl, break the
eggs in and beat with an egg beater. Stir the onion and ham into
the mixture and pour into the pastry shell. Sprinkle cheese over
the top and bake in the oven for 45 minutes, or until the quiche
is set.

serves
4

# Baked Potatoes

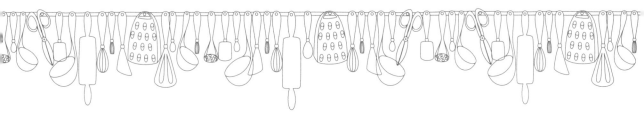

### INGREDIENTS

4 medium potatoes
1 head of garlic
2 rosemary sprigs
butter or sour cream, to serve

### METHOD

Preheat the oven to 200°C/400°F/Gas mark 6.

Scrub the potatoes under running water and prick all over with a skewer or a fork. Add the head of garlic and the rosemary. This stops them exploding in the oven. Put the potatoes at the back of the centre shelf in the oven and bake for 1½ hours.

Remove the potatoes from the oven and, using oven gloves, immediately break them in half. If you leave them whole, the skin goes wrinkly and soft.

Serve with butter or sour cream.

Note: Do not turn the reduce the oven temperature while the potatoes are cooking—they will go soft immediately.

serves
4

# Mashed Potatoes

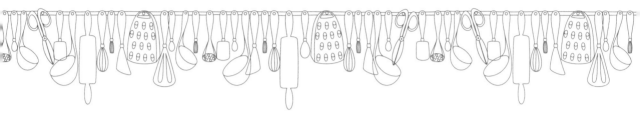

## INGREDIENTS

4 medium potatoes, peeled
125 ml (4 fl oz) milk
30 g (1 oz)
60 g (2 oz) cheese, grated
  (shredded)
salt and freshly ground black
  pepper, to taste

## METHOD

Place the potatoes into a large pan with cold, lightly salted water to cover. Bring to the boil and cook gently, covered, for 20–30 minutes, until the potatoes are easily pierced with a fork. Drain thoroughly, then shake the pan over heat for 1 or 2 minutes until all surplus moisture has evaporated and the potatoes are dry.

Mash the potatoes, then beat with a wooden spoon until very smooth.

In a pan, heat the milk and butter. Once the mixture is hot, add to the potatoes and beat until light and fluffy. Add the cheese and stir through until melted. Season with salt and pepper. Serve immediately.

serves
4

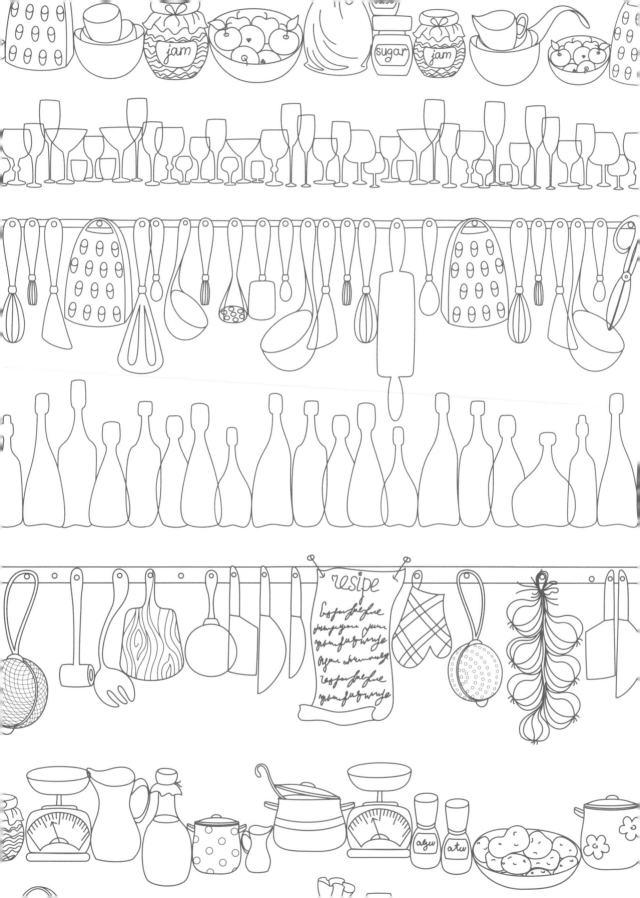

# Pasta, Rice and Noodles

# Cooking Pasta

To cook pasta, bring a large pan of salted water to a brisk boil. Add a small amount of pasta at a time. If you are cooking spaghetti, hold it near the end and gently lower the other end into the boiling water; it gradually softens and curves around the pan as it enters the water. Boil the pasta briskly, uncovered, stirring occasionally until just tender. The Italians call it *al dente* — the pasta should be firm when bitten between the teeth. Do not overcook. Drain in a colander, rinse with hot water and stir through 1 teaspoon of olive oil and salt (optional).

# Cooking Rice

To serve 4 people, pour 400 g (14 oz/ 2 cups) of rice into a large pan of fast-boiling, salted water and boil for 15 minutes, or according to the packet instructions. The rice should be just tender. Drain and serve immediately.

To steam rice, wash 400 g (14 oz/ 2 cups) of long grain rice and drain well in a colander. Place the rice in a pan with 750 ml (1¼ pints/ 3 cups) of water and bring to the boil. Lower the heat to medium and cook uncovered until the water is absorbed. Remove from the heat, empty the rice into a colander and steam over fast boiling water for 25–30 minutes.

# Cooking Noodles

Use fresh Asian noodles direct from the packet, as they are usually already cooked and require no further preparation. If you do need to cook noodles it is a good idea to rinse them in cold water and drain them after cooking to remove the starch. Cook noodles for 2 minutes in rapidly boiling water or follow the packet instructions.

# Mushroom and Onion Risotto

## INGREDIENTS

30 g (1 oz) butter

1 small onion, chopped or
   sliced

1 bacon rasher (strip), diced

12 button (white) mushrooms,
   sliced

300 g (11 oz) arborio rice

375 ml (13 fl oz) chicken stock,
   boiling

125 g (4 ½ oz) cheese, grated
   (shredded)

salt and freshly ground black
   pepper, to taste

fresh herb salad, to serve

## METHOD

Melt the butter in a heavy pan, and fry the onion, bacon and mushrooms, stirring once or twice, for 3–4 minutes. Stir in the rice and cook for 1–2 minutes.

Pour in the hot stock gradually, stirring constantly until the liquid is absorbed. Continue stirring while adding stock until all the liquid is absorbed each time. Cook the rice for 30 minutes, or until it is tender. Add extra hot water or stock, if necessary.

Stir through the cheese, and season with salt and pepper. Serve immediately with fresh herb salad.

serves
4

# Fettucine Alfredo

## INGREDIENTS

50 g (9 oz) fettuccine

125 g (4½ oz) butter

125 g (4½ oz) Parmesan, grated (shredded), plus extra to garnish

¼ teaspoon salt

freshly ground black pepper, to taste

250 ml (8 fl oz) fresh cream

parsley, finely chopped, to garnish

## METHOD

Cook the fettucine for 15 minutes, or until *al dente*, in a large pan of rapidly boiling, salted water.

Meanwhile, melt the butter in a large pan, then add the Parmesan, salt, pepper and cream. Cook over a low heat, stirring constantly, until blended.

Drain the fettucine. Immediately add to the cheese mixture and toss until the pasta is well coated. Place in a heated serving dish, sprinkle with parsley and Parmesan and serve at once.

serves
6

# Fried Rice

## INGREDIENTS

225 g (8 oz) rice, uncooked
250 ml (8 fl oz) water, salted
   for boiling
2 eggs
1 teaspoon oil
250 g (9 oz) lean pork,
   chopped and fried quickly
   in oil
250 g (9 oz) cooked shrimp
   (prawns), chopped
5 mushrooms, thinly sliced
4 shallots, chopped
salt, to taste
4 teaspoons soy sauce

## METHOD

Wash the rice several times in cold water to remove the excess starch. Place the rice in a pan of boiling, salted water and cook for 15 minutes, or until the grains are just tender—do not overcook. Drain the rice and allow to cool completely.

In a bowl, beat the eggs lightly, then heat the oil in a frying pan and fry as a thin pancake or omelette. Remove from the pan and slice into strips. (If you prefer, eggs can be beaten and added to the rice last, instead of frying beforehand.)

Place enough oil in a large pan to cover the base and heat it. When hot, add the prepared rice slowly, to avoid clumping, and stir for about 10 minutes, or until the rice is thoroughly heated through. Stir vigorously, breaking up any lumps.

Add the pork, shrimp, mushrooms, shallots and salt, then fold in the egg pieces (or beaten egg) and soy sauce. Mix well and serve.

serves
4-6

# Spaghetti Bolognese

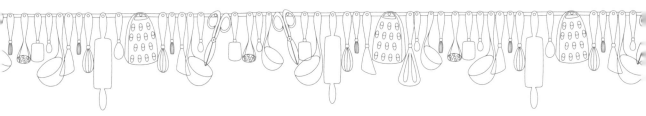

## INGREDIENTS

1 tablespoon olive oil

250 g (9 oz) minced (ground) beef

1 garlic clove, crushed

1 large onion, grated (shredded)

500 g (1 lb 2 oz) tomatoes, peeled and chopped

1 teaspoon oregano or basil

1 teaspoon salt

freshly ground black pepper, to taste

1 teaspoon sugar

3 tablespoons tomato paste

250 ml (8 fl oz) beef stock

250 g (9 oz) spaghetti

Parmesan, to serve

## METHOD

Heat the oil in a frying pan, add the meat, garlic and onion and brown lightly. Add the tomatoes, oregano, salt, pepper and sugar.

In a small bowl, blend the tomato paste with the stock. Add this to the mixture in the frying pan. Simmer for 30 minutes, uncovered, so that sauce thickens slightly.

When the sauce is almost ready, cook the spaghetti in boiling salted water until tender, about 20 minutes, or according to packet instructions. Drain the spaghetti, and place on a hot serving dish or plate. Pour hot sauce over the spaghetti and scatter with Parmesan.

serves
4

# Lasagne

## INGREDIENTS

2 tablespoons olive oil

250 g (9 oz) minced (ground)
    beef

250 g (9 oz) minced (ground)
    pork

1 onion, finely chopped

1 garlic clove, finely chopped

1 teaspoon parsley, chopped

250 g (9 oz) tomato paste

470 ml (16 fl oz) water

½ teaspoon salt

½ teaspoon freshly ground
    black pepper

250 g (9 oz) lasagne sheets

30 g (1 oz) mozzarella, sliced
    thinly

250 g (9 oz) ricotta, crumbed

2 tablespoons romano
    cheese, grated (shredded)

## METHOD

Heat the oil in a pan, add the beef and pork and brown with the onion, garlic and parsley. Stir in the tomato paste, water, salt and pepper and simmer for 1½ hours.

Preheat the oven to 180°C/350°F/Gas mark 4.

In a greased casserole dish about 5 cm (2 in) deep, arrange alternate layers of lasagne sheets, sauce, mozzarella and ricotta cheese. Repeat until the pasta and sauce and two cheeses are all used, ending with ricotta cheese. Sprinkle with cheese and bake for 25–30 minutes.

serves
4-6

# Spaghetti Carbonara

## INGREDIENTS

250–375 g (9–13 oz) fettucine

2 tablespoons olive oil

3 bacon rashers (strips), finely
diced

2 eggs

45 g (1½ oz) Parmesan, grated
(shredded)

250 ml (8 fl oz) fresh single
(light) cream

freshly ground black pepper,
to taste

## METHOD

Tip the fettucine into boiling, salted water and cook for 8 minutes
or until *al dente*.

Just before the fettucine is ready, heat the oil and fry the
bacon.

In a bowl, beat in the eggs and add the cheese.

Drain the pasta and return to the hot pan. Add the cheese
mixture, cream, plenty of black pepper and crisp bacon. Mix
well. Place the pan over a low heat for a minute or so, stirring
constantly.

Place in a hot dish and serve immediately.

serves
4

# Spaghetti with Meatballs

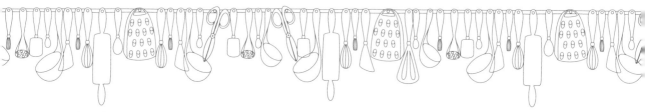

250 g (9 oz) spaghetti

## FOR THE TOMATO SAUCE
1 x 400 g (14 oz) can tomatoes
250 ml (8 fl oz) Italian tomato
  sauce
125 g (4½ oz) tomato paste
60 ml (2 fl oz) water
60 ml (2 fl oz) red wine
2 bay leaves, crushed
2 tablespoons parsley,
  chopped
1 garlic clove, crushed

## FOR THE MEATBALLS
4 slices white bread
500 g (1 lb 2 oz) ground
  (minced) steak
1 tablespoon Parmesan,
  grated (shredded), plus
  extra, to garnish
1 tablespoon parsley, chopped
1 tablespoon onion, grated
  (shredded)
salt and black pepper
¼ teaspoon oregano
1 egg
3 tablespoons olive oil

**METHOD**

To make the tomato sauce, combine all the ingredients in a large pan. Simmer until thick, stirring occasionally for about 10 minutes.

To make the meatballs, place the bread in a small bowl, add enough water to cover, and let stand for 2 minutes. Remove the bread and squeeze out the excess water. In a larger bowl, combine the bread with the minced steak, Parmesan, parsley, onion, salt, pepper, oregano and egg. Mix lightly until thoroughly combined. Shape into small balls. Heat the oil in a frying pan and brown the meatballs on all sides.

Add the meatballs to the sauce and simmer for 15–20 minutes. Meanwhile, cook the spaghetti in salted, boiling water for about 20 minutes, or according to the instructions on the packet. Drain and place on a hot serving dish or plate. Top with meatballs and sauce and sprinkle with Parmesan.

serves
4-6

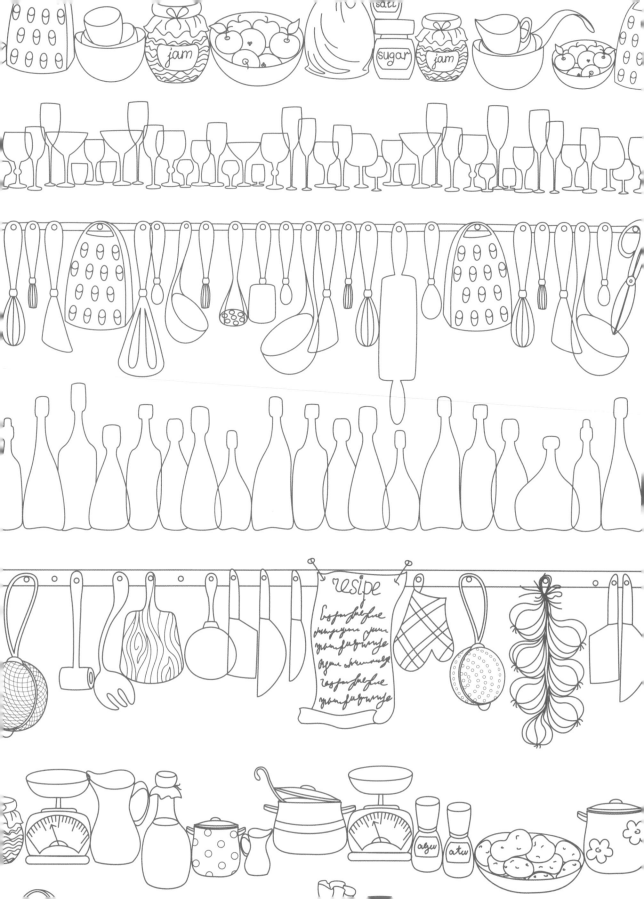

# Fish and Seafood

# Cooking fish

For maximum freshness and flavour, buy your fresh fish on the day you intend eating it—don't store it in the refrigerator for a long time. If fish isn't prepared on the day of purchase, you can freeze it. As a general guide, allow 500 g (1 lb 2 oz) of fish for each person if it includes the head and bones. When the fish is filleted or cut into steaks, allow 125–250 g (4–8 oz) per person, depending on the recipe being prepared and the accompaniments being served.

Most fish shops will fillet the whole fish you buy, but if you prefer to fillet your own, here's an easy way to do it. Make a cut at the back of the head with a sharp, thin-bladed knife. Keeping close to the backbone, cut right down the tail and gently lift the fillet from the backbone using a slicing motion. Remove the fins with scissors. Turn the fish and repeat the process. Remove excess bones from the fillets with a knife or tweezers.

Whichever way you plan to cook your fish, there is usually no lengthy cooking time involved. The moment the flesh is white, moist, and flakes easily when tested with a fork, the fish is ready to eat.

# Grilling (Broiling) Fish

One of the easiest ways of cooking fish is grilling (broiling)—it is also a healthy method of cooking fish. Small whole fish, or steaks and fillets of larger fish and shellfish can all be grilled. Preheat the griller (broiler) to a moderate heat and place the fish on the grill tray to cook. Alternatively, line a grill pan with aluminium foil and cook your fish on the stove top, regularly basting the fish while cooking (combined melted butter and lemon juice is tasty). Herbs, finely chopped onion, white wine or other seasonings of your choice may also be added to the basting sauce. The fish will be cooked in approximately 10 minutes, depending on its size and thickness. Turn the fish once only while cooking as it breaks easily—constant turning is not necessary.

# Frying Fish

Fish may be shallow or deep fried. Deep-frying is ideal for smaller fillets of fish, or shellfish coated with batter. Shallow frying is used for fish fillets or steaks and small whole fish. Always dry pieces of fish well with absorbent paper before cooking. Most fish is coated before frying to protect the delicate flesh and keep it moist. Seasoned flour, or egg and breadcrumbs are two coatings for fish. Use peanut or avocado oil for deep-frying. For shallow frying, olive oil or butter or a combination of the two may be used.

Make sure the oil is very hot before adding the prepared fish. Cook the fish quickly and when golden brown on both sides, remove the fish with a metal spatula or slotted spoon and drain on absorbent paper. Serve immediately while the fish is moist inside and the coating is crisp.

# Coatings for Fried Fish

- Plain (all-purpose) flour seasoned with pepper. (Salt is best added after the fish is fried.) Dry fish well and coat lightly with flour, shaking off any surplus. Small fish may be coated easily by shaking them gently in a plastic bag containing a little flour.

- Egg and breadcrumbs. A deliciously crisp coating for fish. Dip pieces of fish in lightly beaten egg, which has been diluted with a spoonful of water or oil. Coat with fine dry breadcrumbs (or crushed breakfast cereal for a different flavour) pressing the crumbs on firmly. Set aside for at least 15 minutes before frying (the crumbs will then stay on when frying).

- Add freshly ground black pepper, paprika, finely chopped herbs, grated (shredded) Parmesan or other seasonings to the breadcrumbs before coating fish.

- Batter is a delicious coating for fish provided the mixture is thin and light and the cooked fish is eaten immediately while moist inside and the batter is golden brown and crisp.

# Batter for Fried Fish

**BATTER**

60 g (2 oz) self-raising
   (self-rising) flour
15 g (½ oz) butter, melted
125 ml (4 fl oz) lukewarm
   water
1 egg white
¼ teaspoon salt

**METHOD**

Sift the flour into a bowl. Make a well in the centre and add the melted butter and water. Beat together until a smooth batter is formed. Set aside until ready to use. Batter will keep in the refrigerator for 5–7 days.

In another bowl, whisk the egg white and salt together until stiff. Gently fold into the batter and use immediately to coat the fish.

serves
2

# Poaching Fish

Poaching means to cook in a gentle simmering liquid. This method is ideal for whole fish such as salmon and trout, or smoked fish. A fish kettle is ideal for poaching fish. It has an inner perforated tray to place the fish on, and when cooked, the tray can be lifted out without breaking the fish. If a fish kettle is not available, poach fish in a standard large frying pan, but wrap it in a piece of muslin first so that it will not break up while cooking and it can be lifted out of the liquid easily. Salt water, fish stock or milk may be used as a poaching liquid. The fish should be completely covered with liquid while cooking.

Bring the liquid to the boil and immerse the fish. Return the liquid to the boil, then immediately lower the heat until the liquid is just simmering gently. Allow 6–10 minutes per 450 g (1 lb) of flesh. Remove the fish from the pan immediately when the fish is cooked—overcooking means the fish will be soft with little texture or flavour.

# Steaming Fish

An ideal method of cooking delicately flavoured fish or for those wanting an easily digestible food. Fish may be steamed in the upper half of a double boiler (the upper section having a perforated base), over gently simmering water. The fish may be wrapped in aluminium foil to protect the flesh and keep it moist.

Fillets of fish may also be steamed on a greased plate over a large pan of gently simmering water. Season with pepper and dot with butter, if desired. Cover with a second plate. Cooking should take approximately 10 minutes, depending on the size of the fillets.

# Baking Fish

Fish may be baked in the oven either whole or filleted. Most fish are best baked whole, as the outer skin protects the flesh and keeps it moist. There are many delicious stuffings for whole fish baked in the oven. Bake in a hot oven 200–230°C/ 400–450°F/Gas mark 6–7. The length of time will depend on the size of the fish. Either bake in a baking dish and baste with butter and lemon juice while cooking or wrap in aluminium foil, placing small pieces of butter over the fish and a little lemon juice or white wine. The fish is cooked when flesh flakes easily with a fork (test the thickest part of the fish).

Small fillets can be baked in a very hot oven 230–260°C/450–550°F/Gas mark 7–9. They may be coated with seasoned breadcrumbs, grated (shredded) cheese, and sliced tomatoes. But if preferred, dot with butter, add a little lemon juice and baste regularly while cooking. The fish will take approximately 10 minutes to cook. The liquid that drains away from the fish while baking should be used in any sauce being made to serve with the fish.

# Barbecuing Fish

Whole fish, fish steaks, fillets of fish and shellfish can all be barbecued. Whole fish may be barbecued in wire frames, turning frequently. No basting is required, but when cooked and ready to serve, brush the fish with butter and lemon juice and season with salt and pepper. Small fish, freshly caught, may be threaded on stainless steel skewers for barbecuing or they may be cooked in wire frames placed flat over the fire.

Fish steaks, fillets of fish and shellfish may be barbecued directly over glowing coals or cooked in a cast iron skillet or on a hotplate.

# Baked Fish

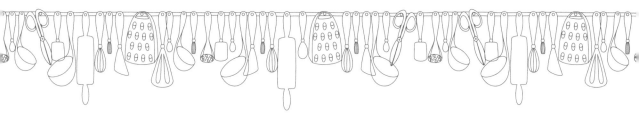

## INGREDIENTS

1 large snapper, mullet or
   redfish, cleaned
salt and white pepper
2 onions, sliced
4 ripe tomatoes, skinned and
   thickly sliced
½ teaspoon ground allspice
¼ teaspoon black
   peppercorns, crushed
½ teaspoon cayenne pepper
2 tablespoons brown sugar
125 ml (4 fl oz) vinegar
60 ml (2 fl oz) water
60 g (2 oz) butter

## METHOD

Preheat the oven to 150°C/300°F/Gas mark 3. Place the fish
in a greased baking dish and season with salt and pepper.
Cover with onion and tomato. Sprinkle with allspice, extra salt,
peppercorns, cayenne pepper and brown sugar. Add vinegar and
water and dot with small pieces of butter.

   Bake the fish in the oven for 20–30 minutes, depending on the
size of the fish. Baste frequently. Serve with a green salad or
vegetable.

serves
4-6

# Garlic Shrimp

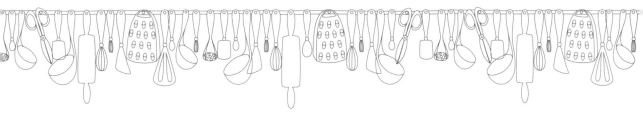

## INGREDIENTS

125 ml (4 fl oz) olive oil

4 large garlic cloves, peeled

1 tablespoon parsley, chopped

½ teaspoon salt

1 kg (2¼ lb) small green
shrimp (prawns), peeled
and deveined

## METHOD

In a bowl, combine the oil, garlic, parsley and salt. Add the shrimp and let stand for 2 hours covered in the refrigerator.

Preheat the oven to 240°C/475°F/Gas mark 9. Place the shrimp and marinade in an ovenproof casserole dish and cook in the oven for 10 minutes, or until the shrimp turn pink. Remove garlic cloves.

Serve as an appetiser on small cocktail sticks, or as an entrée in small ramekins.

serves 8 as an entrée

serves 12 as an appetiser

# Seafood Paella

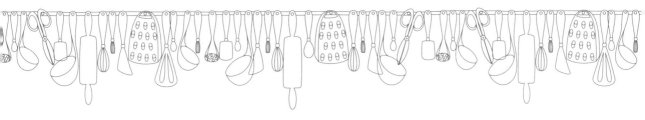

## INGREDIENTS

60 ml (2 fl oz) olive oil

2 tablespoons butter

2 garlic cloves, chopped

1 onion, chopped

1 capsicum (bell pepper),
 seeded and chopped

3 tomatoes, peeled

330 g (11 oz) short grain rice

825 ml (1 pint 7 fl oz) fish
 stock

1 teaspoon salt

¼ teaspoon saffron threads,
 crumbled

mixture of seafood —
 shrimp (prawns), peeled
 and deveined, scallops,
 mussels, uncooked crab

¼ teaspoon freshly ground
 black pepper

3 tablespoons fresh parsley,
 chopped

2 teaspoons fresh oregano,
 chopped

1 teaspoon fresh thyme,
 chopped

## METHOD

In a large frying pan (that has a lid), heat the oil and butter over a medium heat. Add the garlic, onion and capsicum, and cook until tender, about 10 minutes. Stir in the tomatoes and cook for about 5 minutes. Add the rice and stir, then stir in the fish stock, salt and saffron. Cover and bring to the boil, then remove the lid, reduce the heat and simmer for 5 minutes, stirring continually. Add the seafood, then cover and simmer for another 5 minutes. Add the pepper, parsley, oregano and thyme and cook, still covered, until tender, about 10–15 minutes.

serves
8

# Layered Seafood Cream Cheese Dip

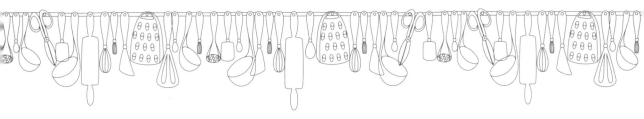

## INGREDIENTS

250 g (9 oz) cream cheese

125 g (4½ oz) sour cream

60 ml (2 fl oz) mayonnaise

175 g (6 oz) cooked shrimp
(prawns)

125–180 ml (½–¾ cup)
seafood cocktail sauce

250 g (9 oz) mozzarella
cheese, shredded

1 green capsicum (bell
pepper), seeds and pith
removed and diced

4 shallots (scallions), finely
sliced

1 tomato, seeded and diced

corn chips or savoury biscuits
(crackers), to serve

## METHOD

In a bowl, combine the cream cheese, sour cream and
mayonnaise. Spread the mixture in a circle over the base of a
serving platter. Layer the remaining ingredients in order over the
top. Chill for 1 hour before serving.

Serve with corn chips or savoury biscuits.

serves
8-10

# Fishcakes

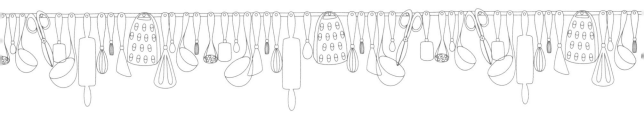

## INGREDIENTS

250 g (9 oz) white fish,
    skinned
150 ml (¼ pint) milk
250 g (9 oz) mashed potatoes
1 egg
salt and freshly ground black
    pepper, to taste
30–60 g (1–2 oz) butter, for
    frying
parsley and lemon, to garnish
salad and lemon wedges, to
    serve

## FOR THE COATING

15–30 g (½–1 oz) plain
    (all-purpose) flour
salt and pepper
1 egg, beaten
3–4 tablespoons fine
    breadcrumbs

makes
8

## METHOD

Cut the fish into chunks, and poach in milk for 8–10 minutes, depending on thickness, and until cooked through. Remove any bones, then flake with a fork. In a bowl, place the fish, mashed potato, egg and seasoning. Mix well, then divide into 8 round cakes.

Put the flour in one shallow bowl and season with salt and pepper. Put the beaten egg in another bowl and the breadcrumbs in a third bowl. Coat each fishcake thoroughly in the seasoned flour, then egg, then breadcrumbs.

Heat the butter in a frying pan and fry the fishcakes for 2–3 minutes, or until golden brown on the underside. Turn, then cook for the same time on the second side. Lift out of the pan and drain on absorbent paper.

Serve hot, garnished with lemon.

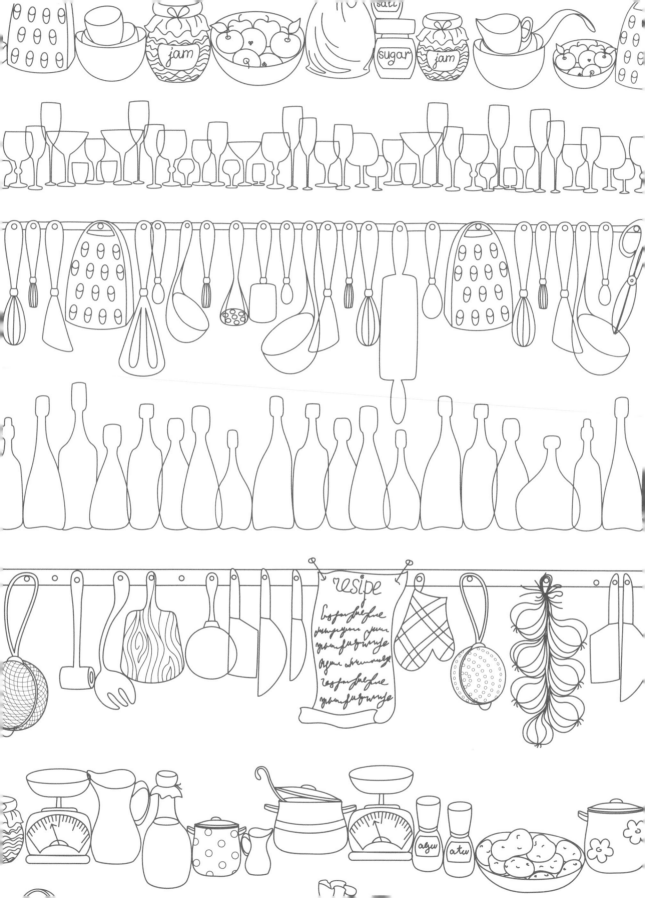

# Chicken

# Chicken Teriyaki

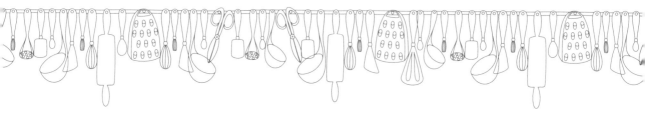

## INGREDIENTS

2 tablespoons butter

75 ml (2½ fl oz) teriyaki or soy
sauce

2.5 cm (1 in) piece fresh root
ginger, chopped

2 tablespoons sugar

2 tablespoons dry sherry

500 g (1 lb 2 oz) boneless
chicken breasts, skinned

8 shallots (scallions), cut into
2.5 cm (1 in) strips

bamboo skewers, soaked in
water

## METHOD

Place the butter, teriyaki or soy sauce, ginger, sugar and dry
sherry in a small pan and stir over a medium heat until the
sugar is dissolved. Leave to cool.

Cut the chicken into 2.5 cm (1 in) pieces and stir into the
marinade with the shallots. Chill for at least 2 hours.

Thread the chicken and shallots onto bamboo skewers and
grill (broil) for 4–5 minutes on each side, or until cooked,
brushing occasionally with marinade.

Serve with steamed rice and salad.

serves
4

# Barbecued Chicken Drumsticks

## INGREDIENTS
12 chicken drumsticks

## FOR THE MARINADE
60 ml (2 fl oz) tomato sauce
2–3 tablespoons lemon juice
2 tablespoons soy sauce
60 ml (2 fl oz) olive oil
½ teaspoon salt

## METHOD
To make the marinade, combine the marinade ingredients in a large non-metallic bowl and mix together well. Put the chicken drumsticks into the bowl, cover and refrigerate for several hours or overnight.

To cook, place under the grill (broiler) or barbecue and cook using medium heat, turning every so often until cooked through.

serves
6

# Satay Chicken Triangles

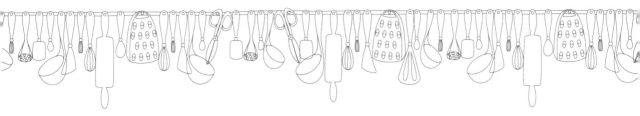

## INGREDIENTS
3 small chicken fillets, diced
20 sheets filo pastry
butter, melted

### FOR THE MARINADE
60 ml (2 fl oz) oil
2 tablespoons white wine
    vinegar
1 tablespoon teriyaki sauce
2 teaspoons sesame oil

### FOR THE PEANUT SAUCE
1 tablespoon tomato ketchup
2 teaspoons chilli sauce
30 g (4¾ oz) smooth peanut
    butter
75 ml (2½ fl oz) chicken stock
2 teaspoons lemon juice

## METHOD
To make the marinade, combine all the marinade ingredients
in a bowl. Add the chicken and marinate for 3–4 hours in the
refrigerator.

Preheat the oven to 220°C/420°F/Gas mark 7. Heat a frying
pan or wok, add the chicken and half the marinade and stir-fry
the chicken for 10 minutes, or until golden.

Brush 1 sheet of filo pastry with butter and top with a second
sheet. Cut the pastry lengthwise into 3 strips. Spoon a portion
of the filling into the corner of one end of a pastry strip. Fold the
pastry diagonally over the filling, from 1 corner to the opposite
side, to form a triangle. Continue to fold the pastry, making
a triangle every time, until the whole strip is used. Brush the
triangle with butter on both sides and put on a baking tray.
Repeat until all filling and all pastry are used. Bake the triangles
in the oven for 15 minutes, or until the pastry is golden brown
and flaking.

In a pan, combine the ingredients for the peanut sauce and
cook for 2 minutes. Allow to cool slightly before serving.

Serve with peanut sauce, for dipping.

makes
30

# Curried Chicken

## INGREDIENTS

60 g (2 oz) butter

1 kg (2 ¼ lb) chicken breast, sliced into 2 cm (¾ in) strips

2 teaspoons curry powder

1 onion, diced

2 bacon rashers (strips), diced

2 carrots, sliced

1 stick celery, sliced

4 oz (115 g) peas, cooked

400 g (14 oz) can tomatoes

1 tablespoon pickles, diced

1 teaspoon tomato sauce

1 teaspoon Worcestershire sauce

## METHOD

Melt half the butter in a frying pan and quickly fry the chicken strips. The chicken should be coloured on the outside, and still pink in the middle. Set aside.

Melt the remaining butter in a frying pan and add the curry powder (use more than suggested if you like your curries hot). Add the onion and bacon and fry for 5 minutes, or until soft. Add the remaining ingredients. If the dish is too dry, add 180 ml (6 fl oz) water with 2 chicken stock cubes dissolved in it. Lastly add the chicken and simmer for 1 hour.

Serve with boiled or steamed rice and condiments such as dessicated (dry, unsweetened, shredded) coconut, cucumber sliced into yogurt and fruit chutney.

serves
6

# Garlic and Herb Chicken

## INGREDIENTS

90 g (3 oz) butter, softened

1 garlic clove, crushed

2 tablespoons shallots, chopped

2 tablespoons parsley, chopped

2 teaspoons prepared mustard

4 chicken maryland (chicken thigh and drumstick) pieces

¼ teaspoon paprika

## METHOD

Preheat the oven to 200°C/400°F/Gas mark 6.

In a bowl, combine the butter with the garlic, shallots, parsley and mustard, and mix well. Carefully lift the skin from the flesh of the chicken, and spread flavoured butter over the flesh. Dust the chicken pieces with paprika, then wrap the chicken individually in baking paper, and then in foil.

Bake in the oven for 20 minutes, then open the foil and baking paper and cook for another 20 minutes.

Serve with tossed salad.

serves
4

# Roast Chicken

## INGREDIENTS

1 x 1.5 kg (3¼ lb) chicken,
   washed and dried
salt and freshly ground black
   pepper, to taste
3 tablespoons olive oil
300 ml (½ pint) chicken stock

## METHOD

Preheat the oven to 180°C/350°F/Gas mark 4. Rub the chicken with salt, pepper and half the olive oil. Truss the chicken and place in a greased roasting pan with the remaining oil. Cook in the oven, basting occasionally, for 1 hour, or until tender and golden brown all over. Remove the chicken and keep warm. While the chicken is cooling make the chicken stock.

   Add the chicken stock to the pan juices and bring to the boil. Strain into a sauceboat and serve with chicken, roast potatoes and green vegetables.

serves
6

# Chicken Satay Sticks

## INGREDIENTS

185 g (6½ oz) chicken
few drops soy sauce
few drops tabasco sauce
1 teaspoon white vinegar
1 teaspoon oil
1 teaspoon brown sugar
1 clove garlic
bamboo skewers, soaked in
  water

## METHOD

Cut chicken into 1.25 cm (½ in) cubes, leaving the fat on. In a bowl, combine the soy sauce, tabasco sauce, white vinegar, oil, brown sugar and garlic. Put the chicken cubes into a bowl and marinate for at least 2 hours in the refrigerator.

Put the chicken cubes on skewers and grill (broiler) very quickly under a hot grill. Serve on the skewers accompanied by a bed of rice.

serves
2

# Chicken Kiev Macadamia

## INGREDIENTS

6 chicken breasts, boned
salt and freshly ground black
    pepper, to taste
180 g (6 oz) chilled butter, cut
    into 6 even chunks
3 garlic cloves, crushed
3 teaspoons parsley, chopped
125 g (4½ oz) plain
    (all-purpose) flour,
    seasoned with salt and
    black pepper
2 eggs, beaten
30 g (1 oz) ground macadamia
    nuts
oil, for frying

## METHOD

Pound the chicken breasts flat with a meat tenderiser. Dust
both sides with salt and pepper and arrange the chicken skin
side down. In the centre of each put 1 chunk of chilled butter, ½
clove crushed garlic and ½ teaspoon chopped parsley. Roll each
breast in toward the centre, then tie each one securely with
string.

Coat the chicken in seasoned flour, dip in egg and then roll in
ground macadamia nuts. Press the nuts on firmly and chill for at
least 30 minutes.

Deep-fry the chicken in hot oil (190°C/375°F) for 5 minutes.
Lift them out and gently remove the string. Return to the oil for
10–12 minutes, or until cooked. Drain on absorbent paper and
serve immediately.

serves
6

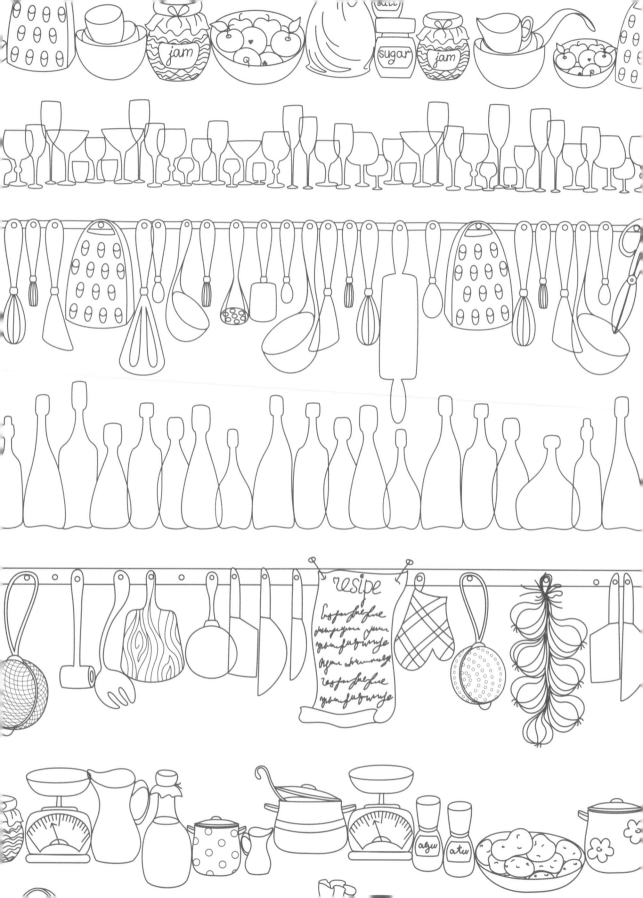

# Meat

# Braised Lamb Shanks

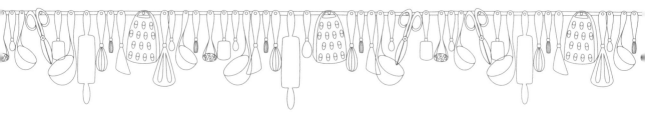

## INGREDIENTS

2 tablespoons olive oil

4 lamb shanks

1 onion, chopped

1 garlic clove (optional), crushed

1 carrot, diced

50 g (1¾ oz) celery, diced

175 g (6 oz) skinned, chopped tomatoes or canned tomatoes

1 teaspoon salt

¼ teaspoon freshly ground black pepper

¼ teaspoon sugar

60 ml (2 fl oz) beef stock, or water

1 teaspoon Worcestershire sauce

## METHOD

Heat the oil in a frying pan and brown the lamb shanks, over a moderately high heat. Pour off most of the oil and reduce the heat. Add the onion, garlic (if used), carrot and celery and cook until the onion is soft. Stir in the tomatoes, salt, pepper, sugar, stock and Worcestershire sauce. Spoon some of the vegetable mixture over the shanks. Place a lid on the pan and simmer for 2 hours, or until tender.

Serve with mashed potatoes and steamed vegetables.

serves
4

# Chilli con Carne

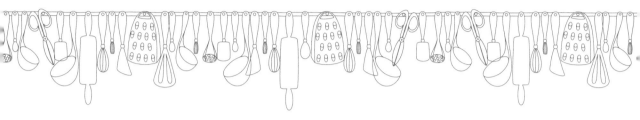

## INGREDIENTS

2 tablespoon olive oil

1 large onion, chopped

1 green capsicum (bell
   pepper), seeds and pith
   removed, and flesh chopped

1 stick celery, chopped

1 tablespoon chilli powder
   (optional)

½ teaspoon salt

¼ teaspoon cayenne pepper

2 teaspoons paprika

500 g (1 lb 2 oz) minced
   (ground) beef

250 g (9 oz) tomatoes or
   625 ml (generous 1 pint)
   tomato pulp

250 g (9 oz) cooked kidney
   beans or soaked and cooked
   haricot beans

150 ml (¼ pint) water

## METHOD

Heat the oil in a large pan. Add the onion, capsicum and celery
and fry until just tender, then add the other ingredients. Bring
just to the boil, then lower the heat and cook gently for about
55 minutes. Stir halfway through cooking, and add a little more
water, if necessary.

serves
4

# Rissoles

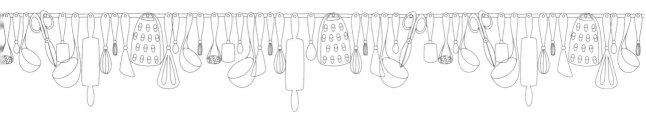

## INGREDIENTS

1 egg

60 ml (2 fl oz) milk

750 g (1 lb 10 oz) finely ground
minced meat

60 g (2 oz) breadcrumbs

1 tablespoon red wine

1 carrot, grated (shredded)

1 zucchini (courgette), grated
(shredded)

1 onion, grated (shredded)

1 teaspoon soy sauce

1 teaspoon Worcestershire
sauce

60 g (2 oz) plain (all-purpose)
flour

1 tablespoon butter

## METHOD

Beat the egg and milk together in a large bowl. Add the mince
and all the other ingredients except for the flour and butter and
mix well.

Spread the flour onto a cutting board. Form the meat mixture
into balls and roll in flour. Then flatten (with a spatula or knife)
into rissoles and place on greaseproof paper. Continue until all
the mixture has been used.

Heat the butter in a frying pan over a low heat. Place the
rissoles in the frying pan and fry for 5 minutes, or until the
bottom is golden brown, then turn and continue to cook for
10 minutes, or until golden brown, on the other side and cooked
through.

Serve with vegetables and mashed potato.

serves
4

# Roast Leg of Lamb

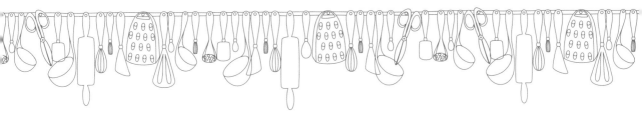

## INGREDIENTS

1 x 1.5 kg (3¼ lb) leg of lamb
salt, to taste
freshly ground black pepper,
   to taste
2 garlic cloves, sliced
2–3 sprigs fresh rosemary

## METHOD

Preheat the oven to 160°C/325°F/Gas mark 3.

Place the lamb in a roasting pan and rub the meat with salt and pepper. Make cuts into the meat and press the slices of garlic inside. Place sprigs of rosemary on top of the lamb.

Roast the lamb in the oven for 1 hour 40 minutes. Basting is not required unless the lamb is very young and has little fat. Season with salt after roasting and let the joint stand in a warm place for 15 minutes before carving.

Serve with roast vegetables, gravy, mint sauce or mint jelly.

serves
4-6

# Roast Pork

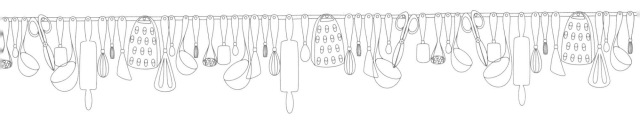

## INGREDIENTS

1 x 3 kg (6½ lb) loin leg of pork
salt, to taste
apple sauce, to serve

## METHOD

Preheat the oven to 240°C/475°F/Gas mark 9. Rub the pork with salt and place in a roasting pan. Cook the pork in oven for 30 minutes to crisp the crackling, then reduce the oven temperature to 160°C/325°F/Gas mark 3 and cook for 3 hours. Continue to baste throughout the cooking time.

When the pork is cooked, place in a carving tray and keep warm. Make gravy from the pan juices.

Serve the roast pork with apple sauce, roast potatoes and roast vegetables.

serves
8-12

# Shepherd's Pie

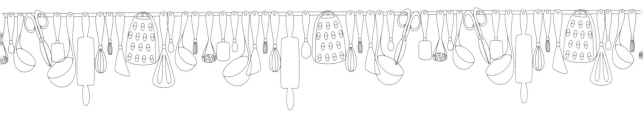

## INGREDIENTS

1 tablespoon olive oil

1 onion, finely chopped

2 tomatoes, skinned and
   chopped

350 g (12 oz) minced (ground)
   beef, cooked

½ teaspoon mixed herbs

salt and pepper, to taste

300 ml (½ pint) beef stock

500 g (1 lb 2 oz) mashed
   potato

30 g (1 oz) butter

## METHOD

Preheat the oven to 190°C/375°F/Gas mark 5. In a frying pan, heat the olive oil and fry the onion for 3 minutes. Add the tomatoes and meat and heat together for 2–3 minutes. Stir in the herbs, seasoning and stock—add less stock if you desire a thicker consistency.

Put the meat mixture into a pie dish and cover with mashed potato. Use a fork to score the top. Dot tiny pieces of butter around on the potato to help it brown. Bake in the centre of the oven until the top is crisp and brown, 30–35 minutes.

serves
4

# Grilled Lamb Cutlets

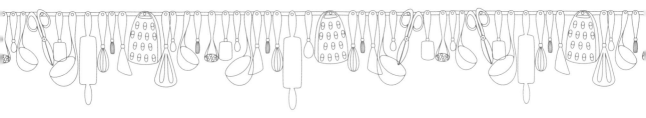

## INGREDIENTS

2 double lamb (Barnsley)
   cutlets
salt and freshly ground black
   pepper, to taste
olive oil, for frying

## METHOD

Trim the cutlets of excess fat and season well on each side.
Put on a rack in a grill (broiler) pan, and brush with oil. Cook
under a very hot grill for 2 minutes to sear the meat. Turn and
sear the other side for 2 minutes. Lower the temperature and
cook for another 10 minutes (turning once after 5 minutes), or
until cooked. Serve with glazed carrots, spinach and mashed
potatoes.

serves
2

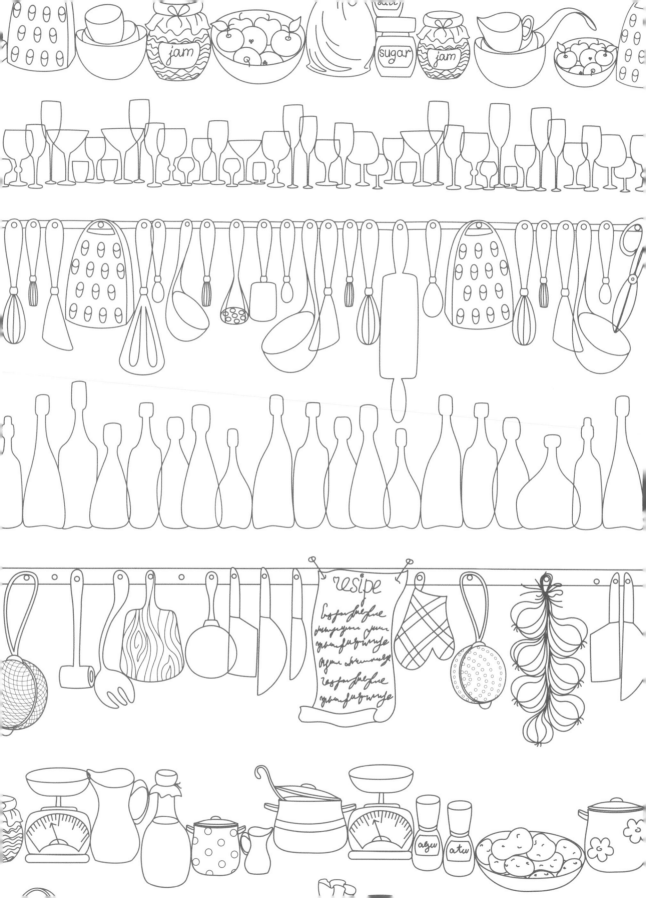

# Desserts

# Apple Crumble

## INGREDIENTS

6 cooking apples, peeled,
  cored and sliced
3 cloves
125 ml (4 fl oz) honey
125 g (4 ½ oz) plain (all-
  purpose) wholemeal (whole
  wheat) flour
100 g (3½ oz) pinhead oatmeal
30 g (1 oz) wheat germ (see
  note)
¼ teaspoon salt
90 g (3 oz) raw sugar
175 g (6 oz) butter
whipped cream or vanilla
  custard sauce, to serve

## METHOD

Preheat the oven to 200°C/400°F/Gas mark 6. Place the apples in an ovenproof dish. Add the cloves and pour over the honey.

Put the flour, oatmeal, wheat germ, salt and sugar in a bowl. Rub in the butter using your fingertips until the mixture is crumbly, then spread the mixture over the apples.

Bake for 1 hour, or until the top is golden brown. Serve with vanilla custard sauce.

Note: Wheat germ is the embryo of a wheat grain. A source of vitamins, minerals and protein. It has a nutty flavour and is very oily. Available from health food stores.

serves
8

# Bread and Butter Pudding

## INGREDIENTS

2 large or 4 small slices of
    bread
butter
60 g (2 oz) dried fruit
sugar, to dust

## FOR THE CUSTARD

2 eggs
1 tablespoon caster
    (superfine) sugar
150 ml (¼ pint) milk, warmed
¼ teaspoon nutmeg, grated

## METHOD

To make the custard, beat the eggs in a bowl with a fork. Beat in the sugar and milk; the milk must not boil, or it will curdle the eggs. Pour into a greased pie dish or basin and top with grated nutmeg. Put the basin into a steamer over very hot water and cook steadily for about 1½ hours. Make sure that the water does not boil—this will curdle the custard.

Preheat the oven to 180°C/350°F/Gas mark 4. Remove and discard the crusts from the bread, then butter the bread thinly. Cut into neat squares or triangles and arrange in a pie dish. Add the dried fruit and pour the egg custard over the top. Allow to stand for 30 minutes. Sprinkle the top with a little sugar and bake for 1 hour. If the pudding appears to be cooking too quickly after 45 minutes, reduce the oven temperature to 140°C/275°F/Gas mark 1.

serves
4

# Carrot Cake

## INGREDIENTS

125 g (4½ oz) self-raising
 (self-rising) flour
175 g (6 oz) brown sugar,
 packed tightly
2 teaspoons cinnamon
115 g (4 oz) carrot, finely
 grated
75 g (2½ oz) raisins, chopped
2 eggs
125 ml (4 fl oz) olive oil, plus
 extra for greasing

## FOR THE FROSTING

30 g (1 oz) cream cheese
30 g (1 oz) butter
100 g (3½ oz) icing
 (confectioners') sugar
1 teaspoon lemon juice
30 g (1 oz) walnuts, chopped,
 to decorate

## METHOD

In a bowl, mix together the flour, sugar, cinnamon, carrots and raisins. Add the eggs and oil and combine thoroughly. Pour into a 20 cm (8 in) greased microwave-proof pan and cook on medium–high for 8 minutes until just cooked. Let the cake stand for 5 minutes.

To make the frosting, beat the cream cheese and butter in a bowl until smooth. Gradually mix in the icing sugar and lemon juice.

Allow the cake to cool then top with frosting and decorate with walnuts, if you like.

serves
6-8

# Cheesecake

**FOR THE BASE**

1 x 225 g (7 oz) plain sweet
   biscuits (cookies)
125 g (4½ oz) butter

**FOR THE FILLING**

250 g (9 oz) cream cheese
75 ml (2½ fl oz) lemon juice
1 x 400 g (14 oz) can
   condensed milk (see note)
whipped cream, to decorate
lemon zest, thinly sliced, to
   decorate

**METHOD**

To make the base, put the biscuits in a plastic bag and seal the
top with an elastic band or twist tie. Using a rolling pin, crush
the biscuits in the bag—you will need to roll again and again.
Pour the biscuit crumbs into a bowl.

Melt the butter in a pan over medium heat, then pour the
melted butter over the biscuit crumbs and mix thoroughly. Tip
the biscuit mixture into a springform cake tin (pan) and spread
it out, then press it down firmly with the back of a spoon. Make
sure you press some up the sides. The biscuit crust should be
about 5 mm (¼ in) thick all over. Put the base in the refrigerator
for 20 minutes while you prepare the filling.

To make the filling, put the cream cheese in a bowl and mash
it up with a fork. Add the lemon juice and condensed milk and
beat until the mixture is smooth. Pour the cheese mixture into
the pie dish and smooth over gently with a spoon. Refrigerate for
at least 4 hours.

When ready to serve, garnish with whipped cream and thinly
sliced lemon zest.

Note: Condensed milk is evaporated milk that has had its water
content reduced, and has been sweetened and thickened with
sugar.

serves
10

# Chocolate Mousse

## INGREDIENTS

2 tablespoons brandy

5 eggs, separated

350 g (12 oz) good quality dark (bittersweet) chocolate, chopped

300 ml (½ pint) double (heavy/ thickened) cream

## METHOD

In a small pan, beat the brandy and egg yolks until smooth. Meanwhile, melt chocolate in a bowl set over a pan of gently simmering water, stirring until smooth. Cool the chocolate, then whisk in the yolk mixture.

In another bowl, beat the egg whites until they form soft peaks. In a third bowl, beat the cream until stiff. Fold the egg whites and cream into the chocolate mixture until no streaks remain.

Spoon into 8 mousse pots or 1 large serving dish. Cover and chill for at least 3 hours, or until set.

serves
8

# Pancakes with Maple Syrup

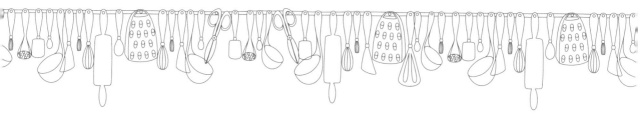

## INGREDIENTS

125 g (4½ oz) self-raising
    (self-rising) flour
¼ teaspoon salt
½ teaspoon bicarbonate of
    soda (baking soda)
250 ml (8 fl oz) milk
3 tablespoons caster
    (superfine) sugar
1 egg
butter, for pan
maple syrup, to serve

## METHOD

Place the flour, salt, bicarbonate of soda, milk, sugar and egg in a bowl and beat together until there are no lumps.

Melt a small piece of butter in a frying pan over a medium heat. Pour a little pancake mixture into the centre of the pan—the mixture should spread out to about 15 cm (6 in) across. Cook until the bubbles on top have burst, then flip the pancake over using a spatula. Cook for another minute or two, until the underside is golden brown, then lift the pancake onto a plate. Repeat until all mixture is used.

As the pancakes are cooked, stack them on a plate, cover with aluminium foil and put in a very low oven (110°C/225°F/Gas mark ¼) to keep warm. Serve with maple syrup.

Variation: Serve with lemon and sugar or fresh berries instead of maple syrup.

serves
8

# Vanilla Creamed Rice Pudding

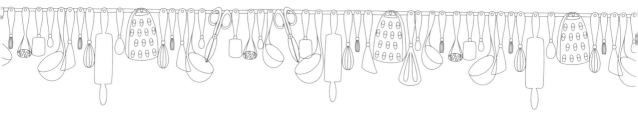

## INGREDIENTS

1 tablespoon short-grain rice

625 ml (generous pint) milk

1 dessertspoon caster (superfine) sugar

1 teaspoon butter

5 cm (2 in) vanilla pod, seeds removed

2 teaspoons ground nutmeg

## METHOD

Preheat the oven to 150°C/300°F/Gas mark 2.

Stir the rice, milk and sugar together in a buttered ovenproof dish. Add the vanilla seeds. Sprinkle the top with nutmeg. Place on middle shelf of the oven and cook for 2–2½ hours. Stir the pudding gently once or twice during cooking, slipping a spoon under the skin to do so.

Serve hot or cold. When serving cold, remove the skin and sprinkle the top with sugar and more nutmeg.

serves
6-8

# Index

First published in 2015 by New Holland Publishers Pty Ltd
London • Sydney • Cape Town • Auckland

The Chandlery Unit 009 50 Westminster Bridge Road London SE1 7QY United Kingdom
1/66 Gibbes Street Chatswood NSW 2067 Australia
218 Lake Road Northcote Auckland New Zealand

www.newhollandpublishers.com

A record of this book is held at the British Library and the National Library of Australia.

ISBN 9781742575629

Managing Director: Fiona Schultz
Publisher: Diane Ward
Editor: Simona Hill
Designer: Lorena Susak
Production Director: Olga Dementiev
Printer: Toppan Leefung Printing Ltd

10 9 8 7 6 5 4 3 2 1

Keep up with New Holland Publishers on Facebook
www.facebook.com/NewHollandPublishers

**UK £12.99**
**US $18.99**